The Upland Farm

1. FARM

February 7

I rose above my common hours to go in search of Thoreau's farm: not the tiny house and lowland farm out at Walden Pond where he made the soil say beans, but the higher ground and upland farm of his inner life where he made his soul say being.

After a gap of decades, I dove again into *Walden* and found myself drawn back into Thoreau's world. But this time I was no mere sojourner; for several years I bathed my intellect in his books and essays, his poems and letters, and his massive *Journal.* Gradually I began to glean the aspirational experiments he pursued at his upland farm, the employment he engaged in on the higher ground of personal improvement and elevation.

By reading and re-reading, by writing and re-writing, I boiled down the sweet sap of his insights; yet I have not stopped at syrup, but have gone on to procuring a few pure crystals of sugar from the new life that stirs in the roots and stems and leaves of his writings. By relating eighteen encounters with Thoreau's life and thought, I have endeavored to embody the transcendent ideals that Thoreau pursued in all his works and days: the true poem of what he made of himself, the form and expression of his entire life, the integrated approach to living that he sought and found, the highest use that he discovered and perfected in his independent existence.

Confusingly, Thoreau hid the approaches to his upland farm behind a thicket of symbols and images. Thus I have found it necessary to seek the meaning of each word and line and passage in his writings, conjecturing a larger sense than the common uses to which he is so often put: the hermit, the gadfly, the political activist, the environmentalist, the advocate for voluntary simplicity.

Although he was all these at times, they do not explain him.

The essence of Thoreau's quest was to pursue an absorbing employment on the higher ground of his soul, to raise a crop that he could barter for heavenly products, to lay a foundation under the castle he had built in the air, to create a moral and intellectual kingdom within himself.

As in the Bhagavad-Gita, the classic of Indian philosophy that he so treasured, in Thoreau's mind the great field to be cultivated is the self, and the greatest achievement is liberation through self-possession, self-control, and self-mastery. Indeed, because the English word "farm" refers to a firm possession and because the Sanskrit word "dharma" refers to a firmly established way of living, it turns out that the upland farmer is a cultivator of dharma!

Yet, even though the upland farm is hard to find, Thoreau provides some clues regarding its location.

First, in *Walden*, he describes how wisdom dictates simplicity of living, independence of mind, grandeur of soul, and trust in yourself — and he associated these virtues with winter, autumn, summer, and spring. There are connections here, too, between these virtues and the stages of life outlined in the Vedic and Yogic philosophies of ancient India.

Second, living as he did in an agricultural society, Thoreau experienced the tensions between the seasons of nature and the seasons of man, and he knew that the ancient Roman writer Varro had categorized the latter as preparing, planting, cultivating, harvesting, storing, and offering for sale. The Roman link triggers associations with Stoic philosophers such as Epictetus and Marcus Aurelius, who also influenced Thoreau in his younger days.

Third, his chosen vocation of natural philosopher led him to spend countless hours observing the botanical stages of seed, sprout, tree, flower, fruit, leaf, and bud; thus he naturally likened those stages to the organic expression of

The Upland Farm

Thoreau on Cultivating a Better Life

The Art of Living, Vol. 4

Peter Saint-Andre

Published by the Monadnock Valley Press,
Parker, Colorado
http://www.monadnock.net/

Cover photo taken at Walden Pond by Amy Meredith
https://www.flickr.com/people/jjandames/

ISBN: 0-9991863-1-0
ISBN-13: 978-0-9991863-1-2

human potential, which must be actively cultivated in order for you to reach fruition as an individual.

Blending these hints, we can see that metaphorically the upland farm is located somewhere between a college town to the east (where you discover self-trust in the springtime of your life), a commercial city to the south (where you pursue grand summer designs of achievement and happiness), a farming community to the west (where you retire from more active affairs and engages in independent, autumnal reflection), and a wilderness area to the north (where you renounce worldly concerns and conduct a life of wintry simplicity).

In his *Journal*, Thoreau notes that even after finding his upland farm, cultivating it was a deeply individual and often lonely pursuit. Not only narrow but rough is the road that leads to the upland farm — only a footpath wide enough for one. There are no mechanical contrivances to be had; instead the upland farmer must work alongside Nature while growing something even higher and better than what she provides.

The true harvest here is that rarest success: to achieve a balance between use and beauty, work and leisure, society and solitude, cooperation and independence, action and reflection, civilization and wildness, the real and the ideal, the practical and the transcendental — between the maintenance of your body and the maintenance of your soul.

Varro considered February 7th to be the beginning of the agricultural year; thus it is a fitting date to begin this journal of encounters with Thoreau — a record of apprenticeship to this master of the art of life, a calendar that outlines the cycles of the day and the year and of life itself. It is only through in-depth exploration that you can get to know Thoreau and to feel at home at his upland farm; yet this short book is only a pocket map of the terrain — a mere sketch of the contours of the land — and is no substitute for reading Thoreau himself in all his beautiful individuality. (A companion book of selections from his writings, *Seasons of Thoreau*, exists to help serve that purpose.)

Furthermore, the pure, hard crystals I have distilled here must be dissolved in the waters of your own life in order to be fully absorbed, and this is a matter of applying Thoreau's ideas and of solving some of the problems of life not only theoretically but practically — for his is a philosophy not only of words but of deeds. As Thoreau said: "We are shown fair scenes in order that we may be tempted to inhabit them, not simply tell what we have seen."

2. SEED

March 11

A seed is a small thing, almost invisible, hardly worth noticing. Yet it is a plant or tree in embryo; it has creative energy and the principle of life and growth within it.

Like the seed is the fruit. If you would eventually bear fruit of a divine flavor, you must pay close attention to learning the origins of your later seasons and to sowing such seeds as sincerity, truth, simplicity, faith, and innocence.

The simplest seed is awareness: awakening to life and its higher possibilities, seeking and finding personal liberation, attuning yourself with serenity and joy to the hope and expectation of greatness. This awareness is a morning invitation to simplicity and innocence, when you throw off the sleep of reason and elevate your life by conscious endeavor. Through a stern simplicity of life and elevation of purpose, you can make your life worthy of the contemplation of your most elevated and critical hour.

Just as bud follows hard upon leaf, so choice follows hard upon awareness. As an upland farmer, you reap what you sow — and you must deliberately select the seeds of your liberation. The seed-time of your character shall produce nobler crops and better repay cultivation than the common stock, for only great and worthy things have any permanent and absolute existence.

Thoreau likened this higher existence to a few particular plants and trees: the flower of the life-everlasting, the arbor vitae or tree of life, and the apples of the Hesperides — a mythical grove that could grant immortality to those who ate its golden fruit (similar to the apples of the Norse goddess Iduna, which enabled the gods to stay forever young).

Choosing to cultivate crops of immortality meant, for Thoreau, living his idealism by hewing to a higher path, maintaining his individuality, keeping his own counsel, getting his living honestly, expecting of himself a nobler course of action in his daily existence. He had faith that these tiny seeds would eventually bear flowers and fruits of immortal beauty — and that, even if he never fully achieved his ideal, the benefits of idealism would accrue to him by producing an unconscious truthfulness and nobleness and beauty of life.

In particular, Thoreau concentrated on three fundamental seeds of a better life and a true success: the seeds of character, of wisdom, and of purity. Just as character is your inner genius settled into place within your life, so wisdom is reason settled and purity is hope or expectation settled. And to be settled means to be nurtured, planted, watered, fertilized, pruned, cultivated, and constantly improved. As in the karma yoga, jñāna yoga, and bhakti yoga of ancient Indian philosophy, you need the yoke of discipline to put these powers into practice and then monitor your progress toward your ideals.

This is how you turn enthusiasm into temperament, how you build the foundation for a higher and more ethereal existence, how you steady yourself for weariless travel on the right road, how you transform the very spring and elasticity of youth into steady upward endeavor toward your distant ideal.

3. PREPARING

March 28

If the seeds of your life are to take root and thrive, you must first plan and prepare. Although Thoreau celebrated wildness, he recognized that the soul is not an unplowed meadow or an uncharted forest, but a garden or an orchard that requires constant tending. As the Stoic philosopher Seneca put it: "Nature does not bestow virtue; it is an art to become good."

So make ready: put on the pack of an upland farmer in good earnest. Know that the tools you can carry are few and small, but ancient and powerful. You must work with your hands, take advantage of what nature offers, and rely ultimately on yourself.

You must also keep your tools sharp: a spade for placing your seedlings down below the mud and slush of opinion and prejudice and tradition and appearance; a hoe for weeding out the many and inevitable distractions of life in modern society; an axe for pruning back the fast-growing branches of your desires and thus for living more simply; a pail for meting out the water of attention onto what truly matters.

In his practical life, too, Thoreau was a collector of only the most essential tools for living as a free and independent worker and thinker. In this way he avoided a mindless consumerism and a bottomless desire for comforts and luxuries.

The upland farmer also requires more rarified skills and aptitudes: mindful attention and being forever on the alert; sincerity and honesty in your dealings with yourself; and a critical eye to sense whether you are ripe or rotten; Stoical virtues such as calm patience, unwearied persistence, and a sturdy discipline; and an endless curiosity about all the varied phenomena of life.

The transcendentalists such as Thoreau used these tools in applying the methods of living they valued most: self-knowledge and contemplation, studious reading in all the great traditions of human thought, and keen observation of nature and society.

Thus does the upland farmer prepare to ply his trade.

4. SPROUT

April 19

Late in life, while studying the forests around Concord, Thoreau noticed that trees which shoot up from stumps or roots are not as vigorous as those which begin in seeds; the shoots inherit the diseases of their parents, whereas the seedlings are thoroughly original and have an organic resilience and elasticity.

Thus the importance, for Thoreau, of developing your own roots and of listening to the faintest but constant suggestions of your own genius. Not for him the grafting of parent stock and the repetition of old errors; instead he preferred to grow resolutely wild and faithful to his own nature, to seek new adventures, to make new discoveries, to try new experiments in living and doing, to cultivate the enterprise and faith to live free.

This is how he approached the year: welcoming the hope and promise of spring, feeling his prospects brightened by the influx of better thoughts, nurturing some innocent fair shoots that would try another year's life — tender and fresh as the youngest plant.

So too did he approach each day: awakening in an atmosphere of divine dreams, rising free from care before the dawn, blessing his whole day with a morning walk, returning again and again to goodness and simplicity, taking pleasure in the most glorious season of the day. As the sun rose he said to himself: "Let us be faithful all round; we will do justice and receive it."

At the lowland farm there are raised beds and greenhouses to protect your seedlings from exposure to heavy rains and late frosts; yet at the upland farm it is not so easy to dodge the pressures of conformity and to maintain your own recovered innocence. It takes a true strength of spirit to spring up and forward with vigor and energy and hope in the future.

For Thoreau, the true harvest of your daily life is to explore your own higher latitudes: the upper regions of thought, the continents and oceans of the moral world, the private sea of your solitude. He turned his back on wealth and power and success so that he could follow his good genius and thus be the king of a celestial empire within. Although he felt sympathy with all living things, his greatest sympathy was with the spirit that animated his own clay and his greatest obedience was to yet more sacred laws and to the laws of his own being.

The germ and kernel of what you will leave behind in the autumn of your life or year or day is to be found in the leaves that sprout in the earliest spring, when the sap runs in your limbs and life buds in your furthest extremities. The impulse and the impetus of your life is found in each moment, for to affect the quality of the day is the highest of arts; and it is through the never-ending accumulation of moments that you feed the countless rootlets forming the foundation of your higher being. Blessed are those who live in the present always, for they remember their creator in the days of their youth and ever see the world with youthful, early-opened, hopeful eyes.

5. PLANTING

May 6

It sounds so easy to follow your genius and obey the spur of the moment. Yet Thoreau recognized that there is a great and deep discipline here.

To plant is to found, to provide with a grounding in the bedrock realities and necessities of life. This is a natural foundation — not a conventional life merely but a human grounding in the very humus of the earth. The seed may fly freely on the slightest wind, but to grow into a mighty tree the seedling must first become deeply rooted.

Thoreau believed that castles deserve to be built in the air, like the eyrie of an eagle that serves as a jumping-off point for this noble bird to sport with proud self-reliance in the fields of the sky. Yet this castle needs a foundation — and what better foundation for such great-hearted pursuits than the topmost branches of the lofty tree of life itself?

To gain strength for this greatest flourishing, you must select and establish the core aspects of your way of life — where you live, how you live, with whom you live — and settle into your choices. By drawing sustenance from the air and sun and soil that surround you, you build the first roots and tender growth of your essence and identity, achieving solidity and structure through a morning faith and trust in the future.

It is one thing to speak of advancing confidently in the direction of your dreams and endeavoring to live the life you have imagined; it is quite another to figure out how to do so. Thoreau always maintained that the right path to a higher experience can be found in a life that is outwardly simply but inwardly complex: in pruning back your desires, weeding out distractions, watering what truly matters. Life, he knew, is a serious business — the kind of private business he transacted at Walden Pond — and the upland farmer will strain every fiber of his moral and intellectual capacity to live in earnest, to attain the right object of living.

Cultivating the upland farm is thus in large measure a matter of renouncing what is unimportant: of knowing what is absolutely necessary for your highest growth and of focusing your energies where they truly count. Yoking yourself to this kind of self-restraint, self-mastery, and self-discipline is essentially similar to the yogic practices of the ancient Indian philosophers Thoreau so admired — for he said that at times even he was a yogin. It is also consistent with the ethics of Stoicism that he imbibed at an early age through his reading of the Greek and Roman classics. Yet this discipline is not imposed from without — it is a higher law nurtured inside, turned over and over in the receptive soil of your essential being, coming near to making a new world within you.

This discipline of securing the most from life starts with what you have: improving from day to day the soil beneath your feet, harvesting whatever crop your life already yields, taking care to watch closely over the fruit of your thoughts and experience. When you do not strain to reach a fruit that is too far beyond your grasp, you slowly shoot upward with ever-expanding confidence; in the same proportion that you root yourself firmly in the earth, so too you rise into the heavens above.

The everyday work of the soul requires a great pile of doing to gain a small diameter of being. One truly experienced moment of life requires countless hours of preparation toward the highest, most elevating goals.

6. TREE

May 20

In the perfect days of late spring and early adulthood, you engage in your first, urgent growth toward your ideals: rooting downward, branching upward, leafing outward.

By focusing on the radicle and root of your existence, you burrow down below the mere surface of things and plant yourself within human nature and the humus of the earth.

By maintaining a scrupulous honesty with yourself, the stem of your identity becomes solid and steadfast.

By pursuing your highest, greenest potential, you increase the genial heat of what you will leave behind later in life and thus provide a benevolent shade to those beneath you.

In these three ways does your spirit unfold — an expansion of the ideal into the actual. You achieve a depth of understanding, a height of character, and a breadth of creativity. You find an abundance of life and health, an everlasting vigor and serenity, and an expectation of perpetual, untarnished morning. You embrace your fate. Instead of experiencing suffering or indifference, you enjoy and bless your existence, and the day and the night are such that you greet them with joy.

The true, living poetry of your life is like this tree, whose leaves precede the flower and fruit. It is what you become through your work; it is how your ideals achieve form and expression in what you leave behind every day and year of your life.

Yet this spring growth into a more rarified air is often checked by the disappointments of experience. Some blast of residual cold threatens the kernel of your life from ripening. The challenge is to not allow such a crisis to keep you from finding your second growth in the autumn of your life, from bearing your fruit at last, from propagating intellectually and morally, from doing the work that only you can do.

It is this that you achieve when you cultivate the tree which you have found to bear fruit in your soil. Although it is tempting to venture far away from your roots in order to achieve greatness, Thoreau counsels that you need not go so far afield to lead a truer life. Instead, keep strictly onward in that path alone which your genius points out. Do the things which lie nearest to you, but which are difficult to do. Live a pure, thoughtful, laborious life, more true to your friends and neighbors, more noble and magnanimous. Thus do you track yourself through life, always on the trail of your deepest nature.

7. TRUST

May 28

For Thoreau, trust was primarily self-trust. Even more important than trusting yourself was to be *worthy* of trust. Ever on the alert for natural and linguistic connections, Thoreau was no doubt aware that trust, truth, troth, and tree share a common root. To be worthy of trust is to be as firm and straight as a tree, to be true to your nature, to be trothed to integrity, to be sincere in your dealings with yourself, to be loyal to a life of principle, to be obedient to higher laws.

These higher laws are the laws of your own being; they are not imposed from without, but are deliberately chosen and obediently followed within. It is the license of your higher being to establish new laws around and within you — such laws as purity, chastity, and temperance. These laws are much harder to live up to than the laws of men, and they point toward the possibility of a divine life. Even though such a life is not open to mere mortals, you can capture some of that ethereal quality by practicing an inward and outward austerity, by letting your mind descend into your body and redeem it, by treating yourself with ever increasing respect. This is partly what Thoreau means by advancing confidently in the direction of your dreams and living the life you have imagined.

By fearlessly living out your own essential nature, you connect your life to the divine — even if the divine is, in the end, unattainable. Few are those who contemplate their highest possibilities, who pursue some crowning experiences above and beyond those that the merely common laws might approve, who generate a revolution in their inner lives.

Devotion to the divine and cultivation of the right way of living require self-restraint, self-discipline, self-governance. There are similarities here to the ancient Indian concept of *brahmacharya* or studenthood: the first phase of life in which you dedicate yourself to deep learning and simple living. You must first train your will, your impulses, and your intellect in order to cultivate the seeds of character, wisdom, and purity.

Developing as it does in the nurturing environment of youth, self-trust might seem opposed to a mature independence. As hinted, perhaps a balance can be found here by imagining the upland farm as located between a college town to the east and a farming community to the west. To find the right away of living, even while building self-trust in your youth you must also seek opportunities for reflection and for thinking independently of your family, teachers, and peers.

Self-trust builds on all the attainments of your early life: aspiration, awareness, deliberation, originality, discipline, self-control, steadfastness, integrity, sincerity. Self-trust is, as it were, the crown of the spring virtues, bursting forth with hope and confidence in the future, sprouting naturally alongside the emergence of self and your own firm identity.

8. FLOWER

June 16

Your roots and stems and leaves — your depth and uprightness and benevolence, and the self-trust that grows from them — provide the foundations for a beautiful and winged life that fulfills your highest hopes and is a blessing to mankind. Thoreau challenges you to achieve a goodness that is not a partial and transitory act, but a complete and constant abundance; when you flow and flower in courage and health and ease, your life gives off a fragrance that is not merely useful, but an unconscious truthfulness and nobleness of character and life that grow gradually from within outward, that inspire those around you, that enhance the general sweetness of the atmosphere, that enrich the world with your visions and joys.

The beauty and purity of which Thoreau speaks comprise the uncompromising principles and consistent self-control that enable you to achieve nobility and magnanimity, to produce works of unsurpassable value, to pluck every flower of thought, to prove every sentiment it is possible to experience. The great task of existence is to get the most from life, to extract honey from the flower of the world. Thoreau urges you to make *that* your every-day business, and to be busy as a bee about it — to be, indeed, both the flower and the bee, both the creator of a perfect summer life and its most industrious gatherer. It is the greatest success to live so that only the most beautiful wild-flowers will spring up where you have dwelt.

To bloom and flourish so exquisitely, you must transcend and translate yourself, as does the caterpillar that metamorphoses into a butterfly. Consider the famous dream of Taoist philosopher Chuang Tzu, in which he wondered how he could distinguish whether he was Chuang Tzu dreaming he was a butterfly or a butterfly dreaming he was Chuang Tzu. In "Higher Laws" Thoreau speculates that the answer might be both: by preserving your higher or poetic faculties in the best condition and by rising above a merely physical, grubbing existence, you can achieve a perfect state of being — a state in which you float freely and happily, sipping the sweetest and most ethereal forms of sustenance while spreading pollen from flower to flower and thus gathering the honey of your higher self.

This metamorphosis, this living up to your highest potential, is inspired most of all by love and by friendship. In love you impart the best of yourself and alone perceive the truest fragrance of the beloved. In friendship can be found the highest fruit which the year may bear, and which lends its fragrance to life. This essential fragrance is the best of ourselves, the ripe thoughts and atmosphere that comprise the crop of crops and that refresh and encourage you not for a moment but for a lifetime. Thoreau found such inspiration in his friend Ralph Waldo Emerson (despite the eventual and perhaps inevitable cooling of their relationship), in Ellen Sewell (to whom he unsuccessfully proposed marriage but whom he still professed to love in the last months of his life), in his brother John and sister Sophia, and in his other close family and friends. Even though Thoreau never married or had children, in many ways he still realized the ancient Indian ideal of the second, active life-phase of *grihastha* by supporting not only his family's household but also for a number of years that of his friend Emerson; and these responsibilities reinforced his highest ambitions.

9. CULTIVATING

July 12

The upland farm requires active care and intentional guidance — for the tree of life needs water and sunlight and air and space to thrive.

Water is like attention: by lavishing attention on what is important, you ensure that you focus on what truly matters. No method or discipline can supersede the necessity of being forever on the alert — especially with regard to yourself, for self-deception is the easiest thing in the world.

Sunlight is like knowledge, especially self-knowledge: by understanding what is possible, you live more earnestly and you receive enlightenment with trust and magnanimity. Although it is true that the sun shines equally upon the lowland farm and the upland farm, the upland light is more regular and pure, since it is unobstructed by the mists and fogs common to the lowlands.

Air is like freedom, for upland air makes free: by pruning back your fears and desires, you cultivate superior virtues and leave yourself more room for expansion.

Space is like solitude: by forming an intimate acquaintance with the weeds that grow in the soil of your life and the vices that grow in your soul, you are more able to pull them up and thus pursue both experiences of significance and opportunities for personal growth.

Cultivating attention and self-knowledge and freedom and solitude — also core values of the ancient Stoics — is the regular work you engage in to hone your being and to nurture a still fresher soul each day. For the soul has a certain magnetism in it, which attracts the power or virtue that gives it life, and which is the motive for all the labor you expend to sustain it. The finest tools you can wield are imagination and reason and belief, which enable a new creation and pasturage of thought within you — the most solid wealth and the most real estate of your life on earth. This is the highest discipline and truest work of the soul, a kind of *karma yoga* on the great field of the self. The motive of one who toils in this field of a wholly new life is do the work well, for the love of the work alone.

Yet, although Thoreau calls you to do some practical work every day, at Walden Pond sometimes he spent the entire morning in contemplation, forsaking works entirely. Even then, however, the day advanced as if to shed light on some work of his. Was there not a tension in his life between the hardworking poet-naturalist (who authored on the order of ten thousand written pages) and the town idler who never held a steady job? He counseled: "Do your work, and finish it. If you know how to begin, you will know when to end." Every day he pursued intellectual studies at his desk and natural studies in the woods and fields. The result was a singular cheerfulness. He was always busy about learning the trade of life, working out a true life for himself — an effort that requires more art and delicate skill than any other employment. Instead of turning out silver by the cartload, he preferred to mine the true, interior gold that was known only to him, high on the uplands of his life — to cultivate the noblest of crops and to get the most honest of livings.

10. MAGNANIMITY

August 6

Ever attuned to the course of the seasons, Thoreau was keenly aware of the longer and cooler nights of August, when the year starts to descend the long slope toward winter. A new urgency accompanies this afternoon of the year: no longer can you afford to postpone the fulfillment of your hopes in a future and anticipated nobleness; instead it is past time to pursue a true life and to take courage in reaching for high flourishing, noble ambition, riotous growth, overflowing life, and a faster progression toward your ideal.

Thoreau called this magnanimity, in its ancient sense of grandeur of soul. He knew that the *anima* is the vital spirit, which forms the basis for character and personality. To be great hearted and high minded is to give no thought and have no need for mere ornament, but to accept an invitation to be what you are —something noble and worthy. The upland farm will produce nobler crops, and better repay cultivation in the long run.

The great challenge, in the afternoon of life, is to nurture an atmosphere of perpetual morning, to sustain the great expectations of your youth, to reinvigorate and reform the very medium of your existence, to maintain your life with dignity and sincerity, to burst the bonds of despair and realize the full grandeur of your destiny, to find elevation in every hour, to exercise your highest human faculties — to make your life, even in its details, worthy of the contemplation of your most elevated and critical hour. It is to advance into the career of life with the equanimity of nature, silent and patient and unpretending; to move onward through your midday with earnest toil and a lofty and serene countenance; to prepare, through the accumulated deeds of the day, a rich western blaze against the evening of your life — to have a fresh dawn, and a great noon, and a serene sunset in yourself.

In the summertime of life and the royal month of August, you spend your greatest life energy in an outdoor life that is all for action. Yet Thoreau counsels that there is no need to venture far from the core and heart of your life in some frontier country: instead cultivate the field on which you find yourself, and do the things which lie nearest to you but that are difficult to do. It is more than enough to breathe your self, to give voice to a free life and free expression without bounds, to rise above sects and parties. The essence of your person can be found in your best thoughts; by having the self-discipline to honor them, you honor the freedom to think sacredly and create devotedly — a freedom from fear, from disturbance, from prejudice, from external constraint. When you honor the immutable laws of integrity and magnanimity, you hold to an inward light and appreciate the noble deeds that can be done on this earth.

Thoreau went to Walden Pond to transact some private business, and to do so greatly and unhurriedly. He avowed that when you are unhurried and wise, your perceive that only great and worthy things have any permanent and absolute existence, that petty fears and petty pleasures are but the shadow of reality, and that your proper pursuit and high calling is to root yourself firmly in the earth so that you can in the same proportion rise into the heavens above. When you do so, you live in relations of truth and sincerity: a pure, thoughtful, laborious life, more true to your friends and neighbors, more noble and magnanimous.

This active pursuit of a noble life is the seeming opposite of the simplicity that Thoreau so cherished. Yet in the end it is congruent with his knowledge and acceptance of the seasons. The cycles of work and rest, growth and harvest, are just as natural to the day and the year of the individual as they are to Nature herself. No one part of the cycle of life provides complete fulfillment; and if in the summer of life you approach the upland farm from a commercial town to the south, bustling with activity and ambition, this too is but one direction and path to a higher existence.

11. FRUIT

September 2

Having adventured on life in the high summer, having sent your shoot upward with confidence, it remains to mature and ripen, to come to your growth and fruition — for the nobler plants are valued for the fruit they bear at last in the air and light, far from the ground, unconsciously acting for the best and noblest ends, seeking for nothing else but to live.

To be ripe is to be perfected and to serve a transcendent use — not a means to a higher end, but an end in yourself, such as the transcendent use of Thoreau's great hero John Brown. It is to have some spare capital and abundant vigor in respect to your spirit and imagination, a true wealth and independence, a free and adventurous soul, a reserve of elasticity and strength, and a good genius that transmutes your whole life into purity and devotion to your highest ideals. When everything about you glows with maturity from roots to stems to leaves, when you are no longer dependent on your transient moods, when all your experience mellows into wisdom, when everything you have been and have done in the spring and summer of your life bears its fruit — then you are ripe at last.

This fruit is the successful realization of your highest potential, your true nature, your inner seeds of character, wisdom, and purity — not a delicious and ephemeral springtime fruit like the strawberry, but a lasting food that is hardened by the sun of summer and the coolness of autumn. The ripening of this fruit means to be well employed as the person you are. When in *Walden* talks about lives of quiet desperation, he does not speak to those who are well employed — as long as they know that they are well employed.

But there's the challenge: how do you test yourself for ripeness and know whether you are making full use and enjoyment of the finest qualities of your nature, whether you are maturing your finer fruits, whether you are addressing a higher taste for ethical beauty?

One clue is whether you are living simply and wisely, whether you have a serious eye and a sincere life. Your proper and finer work is a true integrity day to day, and too often you are prevented from doing this work by a lack of moderation and self-control, occupied as you are with trivial concerns and coarse labors. Your highest fruit is not your economic use — for most people exaggerate the importance of the work they do — but a more spiritual employment and a set of more essential, ethereal qualities: transparent character, constant abundance, and simple humanity. It is a matter not of having something to do, but of having something to be. The ambrosial and essential part of the fruit, its true flavor, is imparted only to the one who raises and plucks that fruit for its own sake — for it is too pure to have a purely market value.

Another clue is whether you are plucking the golden apple of the Hesperides — the apple of the tree of self-knowledge. Is your primary trade with the celestial empire that produces this finest fruit? Such trade requires strict business habits, and labors that task your highest human faculties: persistence, strength, enterprise, bravery, serenity, alertness, adventurousness, confidence, and courage. As Confucius observed: "You must know that you know what you know, and know that you do not know what you do not know." You must test and observe yourself closely, with as much honesty and sincerity as you can muster, in order to know whether you are truly ripe, whether your inward verdure is that of a wholly new life.

The fruit of these efforts tastes all the sweeter and more palatable for the very difficulties you have contended with in reaching it.

12. HARVESTING

September 18

The ripening of existence, the late and perfect maturity of experience, imparts a certain mellowness and stronger flavor to life. It is time to harvest your ripened fruits, to reap what you have sowed, to pluck the days and works of your achievements, to appreciate the beauty of your life with an Indian-summer serenity even in the face of joy or sorrow, past or future, pleasure or pain.

The true harvest of your daily life is, like the most subtle tints of morning and evening, a gratitude for existence, a simple and irrepressible satisfaction with the gift of life — like a calm September afternoon in which the surface of a woodland lake is as smooth as glass.

This is the pure liquid bliss of a serene happiness, not animated by the thrills of an agitated joy or frenzied delight, but a wonderful purity attained by being reserved and austere, by living with gentleness and a humble gratitude for the fruit of character which feeds you and the tree of life which shadows you, by practicing justice and innocence and a greater humanity.

This is a gratitude not only for rest, but also for toil; a harvest not only of the sweetest fruits, but also of the scarlet leaves of the thoughts and acts you planted in the seed-time of your character, which have acquired consistency and hardness, a concentrated flavor, and a mellow ripeness. You must gather that rich crop of experience which your life yields; you must confidently and heartily live up to your ideals — for if you are in error you will learn, and if not you will improve.

Do not spend your time atoning for the neglect of past opportunities, but even in the evening of your works and days allow your prospects to brighten on the influx of better thoughts and a rejuvenescence and faith in the current time. As with the hero Arjuna in Thoreau's treasured Bhagavad-Gita — the great archer who was able concentrate so deeply that he could always hit the target — so the wise person focuses on the present moment as the single point at which life ever happens. For the Stoics, as well, a focus on the present was the key to happiness.

Daily recover your innocence through serene work in the true field of life and self. Live in the present with a pure morning joy — for this season, too, is a season of growth, a second spring. Launch yourself on every wave. Find your eternity in each moment. Know what game to play today, and play it. Postpone no opportunities. Look not to some other land; for there is no other land, no other life. Take any other course and life will be a succession of regrets. Harvest as early as possible if you would escape the frosts.

If you are not happy on harvest day, you will not be so tomorrow. And is not every day a harvest day?

13. INDEPENDENCE

October 5

The ripeness and maturity of your fruits are a reflection of the vividness and color you achieve in the peak of your character. When you grow above and beyond the soil in which you were planted, you require nourishment less from the earth than from the more ethereal elements of sun and air; when you reflect upon the rich crop of your experience, you commence a more independent and individual existence; when you put the world behind you and are pledged to no institution in it, you realize that you are self-dependent, self-governing, self-reliant, self-derived. You achieve your true character; you come to know the prince-like nature of the soul; you become what you are.

A natural independence of thought and action consists of earnestly seeking the right way of life, standing upright and reaching ever higher, fronting the facts as you perceive them, finding encouragement and inspiration beyond the present condition of things — in ageless principles, in higher things, in the buds of the future, in your best possibilities. Such wisdom is attained not through mere experience but through reflection: living and thinking not habitually and conventionally but with open eyes and clear awareness, seeking not routine but a rooting in the fundamentals of existence.

This pursuit of a higher and more universal life frees you from all enervating luxuries. Thoreau found this freedom in simple, honest, independent labor, especially in his time alone at Walden Pond, when he also worked occasionally as a day laborer; yet he did not claim that this was the only path — only that it was his path. He counsels you to be very careful to find and pursue your own way, not that of your parents or peers or neighbors or even Thoreau himself. His advice is to not let your work or your manner of living become a hindrance to your true course and highest goal in life, to an everyday heroism and even holiness.

Cultivating a heroic spirit and a universal life requires seeking out remoter retirements and more rugged paths: great and worthy things that have a permanent and absolute existence, not petty fears and even pettier pleasures. Similarly, apprehending what is true and noble and sublime requires undisturbed solitude and stillness, self-directed reflection and contemplation, and an unhurried wisdom. Yet it is not that Thoreau necessarily loved to be alone, but instead that he loved to soar so high that he left his companions behind.

Nowadays we think of retirement as financial independence, so that you can travel the world or check off the items in list of conventionally appealing activities. In ancient Indian philosophy, the life-phase of retirement or *vanaprastha* was more a matter of gradually withdrawing from the active affairs of life as you turn toward spiritual liberation. This is more in line with Thoreau's thinking: to be wealthy and independent in respect to your spirits and imagination, to have spare capital and abundant vigor, to retain a reserve of elasticity and strength so that you can be liberated from ordinary limits. If you are not cramped by spiritual debts, you have the freedom to spend your time and energy on the highest pursuits, to enjoy the gift of life and taste its deepest flavor.

14. LEAF

October 17

Just as the earth expresses itself outwardly in leaves, so you express yourself outwardly in your actions. Just as the leaf, having been perfected, leaves the tree and has its own independent existence, so your actions, having been perfected, leave your soul and have their own independent existence. Just as in the economy of Nature nothing is wasted, so in your life everything is put to use, every decayed leaf and twig and fiber of your being serves as compost for your future growth.

The true poem of your life is a new creation: what you have become through your work, through the pursuit of your highest use, through seeking to bring a transcendent idea into form and expression. Although this poem is the spiritual inheritance that you leave behind, it is built up from something more prosaic, for you nourish the roots of your being with a natural fertilizer formed of the slough and dross of your daily experience. Each day brings new leavings, new opportunities for learning from your mistakes and your successes, new chances to read of others' experiences in the form of biography and history and philosophy, as well as your own experiences of friendship and family and social observation.

The change to some higher color in a leaf is evidence that it has arrived at a late and perfect maturity. When you do what you do best or most perfectly, what you have most thoroughly learned by the longest practice, what has sprung from seeds planted early in life, then your actions fall from you effortlessly, as the leaf falls from the tree, with abundance and an unconscious philanthropy that grows organically from the energy and benevolence of your first spring shoots.

A successful life is a complete maturity, a ripening from root to stem to leaf, when your entire being blooms as one flower — when you finish your summer's work, ripen your seeds, rejoice in your existence, experience unalloyed reflections, faithfully discharge your duties, neglect none of your economies, add to your stature in human virtue, and show that you have grown steadily toward heaven all through your life.

When you have lived thus well, you can lie down and take leave of life as gracefully and contentedly as the leaves do when they fall from the trees in autumn; your works and days are an anticipation of spring, an evidence of warmth and genialness, a preparation for passing from this life into another. In the Indian summer of a finer atmosphere and a pensive beauty, you experience pure and distinct reflections, your thoughts are a foretaste of the spring, and you find a time of Oriental contemplation, of faith and serene confidence.

15. STORING

November 17

Thoreau counselled to provide for coming dormancy on cold November days by cultivating a renewed focus on the essentials of life. Put things on a winter footing and find a certain broad pause and opportunity to start again, to turn over a new leaf even after the few remaining leaves of summer have come fluttering down.

Yet the prospect of winter does not lead to a bleak and cheerless resignation, because the true harvest of the day, of the year, and of life is to be found not in the sweet, ripe fruit which it yields, but in the concentrated, nutty kernel of thought which it occasions. This is a matter not of plucking each fruit as it passes, but of gathering a rich crop of experience and growth, cheerfully threshing the grain and separating the kernel from the chaff, picking over the choicest specimens of what you are and aspire to be, and storing these safely away.

Make a faithful record of your strivings and learnings, the things you love to think of, your affection for any aspect of the world; in so doing, you store each of these for future use and can restore it again at will through the faculty of imagination. The reminiscence affects you as poetry and enables you to appreciate the experience and mood of that other season of life, whatever it may be. Thus only the rarest flower and the purest melody of the season comes down to you. The world so seen is all one spring, full of beauty.

It is never too late to slough off your errors and give up your prejudices, to insist upon proof for your ways of thinking and doing, to purify yourself of the dross and earthiness which you have accumulated during your experience of life.

Aspire to practice in succession all the honest arts of life. Late in the day, the best of these is sincere and searing reflection: to settle your accounts, to admit whether or not you have lived deliberately and have been well employed, to give tone and firmness and consistency to your thought and actions. The same practice was prevalent among the ancient Stoics, who in the evening would meditate on the events of the day and reflect on how they went wrong, and on what they did or left undone. If in your most elevated and critical hour you find your life and behavior unworthy, let not your experience wear upon you, but, encouraged, set out again to climb the mountain of the earth and seek a future that is worth expecting.

Yet this discipline of self-knowledge is, like the jñāna yoga of the Yogic philosophy, not a matter of constraint and severity. Thoreau may have been a sort of natural Stoic, but his was a cheerful wisdom. He learned to live, to make few apologies, to be resolutely and faithfully what he was, to be humbly what he aspired to be.

16. SIMPLICITY

December 7

Thoreau emphasized over and over the importance of simplicity: having few wants, focusing on your true needs, being earnest and sincere, concentrating on the essential laws of existence, magnanimously accepting what nature has given you. Yet simplicity is not an end itself, but always a way of clearing the land for engaging in some absorbing employment on your higher ground, for building up an inner wealth of spiritual insight, for investing in your higher self and letting your capital be purity, serenity, and contentment.

These serene moments are merely a transient realization of what might be the whole tenor of your life. The highest development and employment is simplicity through wisdom and the cultivation of the highest faculties. If yours is an ant-like existence of working for common luxuries and superficial refinements, or even if you live for knowledge and culture as conventionally defined, you have no time to experience profound thoughts and inward complexity. Outward complexity is enslavement to trivial desires, whereas voluntary simplicity is freedom for pursuing a better character and a higher, nobler life.

Attending overmuch to routines, conventions, manners, events, and other trivialities dissipates and impoverishes the mind, robs you of strength for things of ageless importance, and keeps you from the unfolding of your higher self. Life is frittered away on a thousand details and distractions, on luxury and heedless expense of time; this is the place to exercise a rigid economy and an honesty and elevation of purpose, so that you concentrate your energies on your two or three pursuits of greatest value, or ply a single heavenly trade with the celestial empire. Thus can you become a master workman of the art of life.

This stern and more than Spartan simplicity of life, this seeming poverty of excitements and experiences, this withdrawal from human society and worldly concerns, this pruning of your hopes to the bare essentials, is in fact a concentration of strength and energy and flavor that fits you for spiritual abundance and a higher society — the sweet friendship of the seasons, the most innocent and divinely encouraging society in every natural object and in universal nature. For heaven is under our feet is well as over our heads, and can be found in simple and homely things, in the most common events, in the everyday phenomena of nature. When the questions to be decided are as simple as how to do your work and live your daily life, then you realize that your natural wants are easily and gracefully satisfied.

According to Thoreau, most people satisfy their wants in a complicated, indirect, artificial way; trading their time for money and their money for the goods they need, they postpone instant life and miss out on the inexpressible joy that is the reward of satisfying their wants simply, directly, and truly. The real arts of life — such as growing and cooking your food, collecting your fuel, building and maintaining your shelter, making your tools, conveying yourself under your own power, and, when temperately pursued, getting the means of your living — are simultaneously your work and your highest pleasure. The warmth of life is not so much in having the necessities as in getting them through simple, honest, independent labor.

Few people live this way today, as modern life rushes headlong in ever more complex directions. Indeed, Thoreau is commonly thought of as an atavistic inhabitant of a far northern wilderness, who left behind all human society consistent with the ancient Indian ideal of *sannyasa* or renunciation.

Yet even Thoreau did not live most of his life this way; after his two years at Walden Pond he returned to live with his parents and sisters, and often helped with the family's pencil-making company. Despite his engagement in the active business of life, he felt that it furnished nothing on which the eye of reason could rest — and that a simple, wholesome, true relation to nature grants you health and happiness and inspiration and a hundred other far finer and nobler fruits than the mere products of human enterprise.

This is why he thought that his true calling was to explore the natural environment around Concord, to earnestly educate himself in that economy of living which is synonymous with philosophy, and to write the poem of his life so well that it would be a source of inspiration to future generations.

17. BUD

December 22

Even though bud and Buddha are etymologically
unrelated, they are conceptual cousins, for in Sanskrit
buddhi is the faculty of awareness or consciousness, which
alone makes wisdom possible through discernment of
truth from falsehood, good from bad, virtue from vice.

Thoreau believed that, despite all your experience of life,
you can to attain a recovered innocence through the love
of virtue and the pursuit of perfection (constantly
improving your soul by removing its impurities, constantly
refining your life by fitting yourself for a finer society);
that, despite being old in years, you can be young in soul;
that, despite the jarrings of life, you can hold on to
freedom and peace in your mind, and find stillness inside
so that you can reflect the beauty of both cultivated and
uncultivated nature; that, despite the coldest and bleakest
winter, you can keep a summer virtue in your heart.

In relation to virtue and innocence and your highest
possibilities, the buds and hidden shoots of winter are
unexpanded — you are ever green and full of sap, and it is
earliest spring with you. The bud sleeps patiently with faith
in an unseen spring, yearning for an unceasing growth, for
a more advanced and still advancing youth. On the pensive
shores of evening, the bud of imagination contains within
itself the hope and expectation of a seed-time whose
bright and immortal harvest cannot fail. Forming these
buds for the next season of growth is the real purport of
your toil, the true kernel of what you bring to fruition, the
final fruit of your day's and year's and life's work.

The swelling but seemingly resting bud extends the
continuity of life into the next season of growth. Like the
apples of Iduna, it is the symbol of perpetual youth. At
the end of each day or year, the wonderful purity to be
found in the ideal of a wise and sturdy innocence is a

recognition of the possibilities for tomorrow or next year — of what you still need to do in order to achieve your ideals. Even at the end of your earthly existence, it is a bravery and confidence about the future of humanity, for our human life but dies down to the root and is never fully eradicated. The brave spears of the next season's buds do not succumb to melancholy, nor do they despair of life; instead they confidently shoot upward and forward to a future unfolding of character, when the living green blade will reach again for eternity. Indeed, the next season of your own growth could be posthumous, as in the arc of Thoreau's growing fame and influence even two hundred years after his birth.

The ever-expanding love of what is best is the summation and transcendent use of your life: to climb above even your upland farm to achieve a budding ecstasy on the highest plane of your existence. And you can attain these soaring heights by living ever in the present moment with complete attention and deliberation. If you can interrogate each impulse to determine if it is in accordance with your higher nature, if you can deliberately affirm or deny each desire in a moment of reflection, then you can act with full intention on those impulses and desires that you have consciously affirmed. Indeed, this interposition is the essence of being human. Yet, when used in service of the most transcendent ends and goals, it is also the essence of philosophical practice: by nurturing the seeds of character, wisdom, and purity within you, you can progressively make your life consistent with your highest hopes and expectations; by so loving wisdom as to live according to its dictates, you can achieve a life of simplicity (because you act on fewer desires), independence (because you judge by the light of your own reason and ideals), magnanimity (because you continually desire higher and better things), and trust (because through these disciplines you become true to your best self).

18. OFFERING

January 6

Just as the Bhagavad-Gita emphasized devotional service and an offering of yourself to what is highest and best, so Thoreau was devoted to the discovery of divinity in nature, in other people, and in himself. This reverential attitude towards life, reached through a long process of spiritual maturation, results in a beautiful life and a transparent character. It is essentially similar to the *bhakti yoga* of Yogic philosophy — the discipline of devotion.

Yet Thoreau did not believe in completely selfless duty or action without recompense, any more than he believed in selling your soul for external things and worldly success. Instead, he believed that there is a certain volatile and ethereal quality which represents your highest value, which is too pure to have a purely market value, which cannot be bought and sold like the grossest groceries. The richest gifts you can bestow are the least marketable by conventional standards; the best of your wares are a real and earnest life, a sincerity and plainness in how you live, and a spending of your life energy on higher works. If you follow your genius and cultivate the best within you, you can raise a crop which you need not bring down to sell at a lowland market, but which you can barter for the heavenly products of the celestial empire.

To create these heavenly products, is it necessary to believe in a traditional god? Although Thoreau was not a churchgoing person, he saw divinity within and behind all of nature. At the end of his life, one of his aunts asked him if he had made his peace with god, to which he replied: "I did not know that we had ever quarreled." Perhaps Thoreau's pantheism and his faith in the seeds of goodness within each human being lead essentially in the same direction as Jesus when he said that the kingdom of god is within you.

Thoreau argues that it is a vulgar error to suppose that you can taste the higher flavor of life without having done the hard, sometimes lonely work of preparing, planting, cultivating, harvesting, and storing. Making a free offering of your work and energy leads to the rarest success: supporting simultaneously both your body and your essence. This is not only a transcendent use but also a complete enjoyment, for the spirit with which you do something determines whether it is a truly fruitful experience and whether it contributes to your development as a human being. Achieving a harmony of your work and your life makes you fully alive and gives your days an inexpressible satisfaction, a sense of elevation and expansion, a feeling of participation in that which is immortal.

In *Walden*, Thoreau speaks of so loving wisdom that you live according to its dictates: maintaining yourself by honest means; living and thinking independently; pursuing magnanimity on a higher plane of life; making and remaking an inner world by turning and returning to what you essentially are; weighing and settling and gravitating toward that which most strongly and rightfully attracts you; traveling the path that only you can travel; being resolutely and faithfully what you are; loving your life so deeply that you meet it and live it every day; knowing that the goal is distant and upward and worthy of all your life's efforts to achieve.

Treating your life as an offering to what is best and highest is to make your life a true sacrament, a dear and cherished object that you constantly improve. Like the artist of Kouroo at the end of *Walden*, you too can find life everlasting and perennial youth through the polished purity of your soul and your works, from singleness of purpose and resolution toward a more transcendent ideal.

Even at the end of life, dawn breaks and the sun rises. The springtime of the day merely presages the perfect summer life to which you can aspire in your highest hour, which you can cultivate at your upland farm; for human beings can also rise to a beautiful and winged life, and you too can become what you are, having learned what that is.

For Further Exploration

If you enjoyed *The Upland Farm*, here are some other works you might like:

- Philip Cafaro, *Thoreau's Living Ethics: Walden and the Pursuit of Virtue*

- Paul Friedrich, *The Gita within Walden*

- Robert D. Richardson, *Henry Thoreau: A Life of the Mind*

- Ethel Seybold, *Thoreau: The Quest and the Classics*

The Upland Farm is the fourth volume in a six-movement suite of books I'm writing on the art of living:

1. *The Tao of Roark: Variations on a Theme from Ayn Rand (2012)*

2. *Songs of Zarathustra: Poetic Perspectives on Nietzsche's Philosophy of Life (2018)*

3. *Complete Yourself: Aristotle's on Personal Excellence (forthcoming)*

4. *The Upland Farm: Thoreau on Cultivating a Better Life (2017)*

5. *Letters on Happiness: An Epicurean Dialogue (2013)*

6. *Gods Among Men: A Novel of Pyrrho and Alexander the Great (forthcoming)*

www.ingramcontent.com/pod-product-compliance
Lightning Source LLC
Chambersburg PA
CBHW071649040426
42452CB00009B/1815